MYRICS

ONE ONE HUNDRED

FEBRUARY 12, 1966

H. C. Berglund

AUTHOR / ILLUSTRATOR

Christopher Richard Andler
March 20, 2023

I'm just a dude

Who loves his brood

Unknown poetry prone

Unaware poetry fair

Blind poetry mind

Cloaked poetry spoke

Clueless poetry knewness

Blindsided poetry coincided

"AN OPEN MIND

WILL HELP YOU FIND"

Me...

Contents

AUTHOR / ILLUSTRATOR i
CHAPTER ONE
   THE UNIFIER 1
HONEST ABE 3
VERSE CURSE 4
LIBERTY BELL 5
IN MIDDLE RIDDLE 6
NO ONE IS WITHOUT FAULT 7
INDIG 8
BoL OF BULL 9
THE ADVOCATE 10
RELIGION DIVISION DERISION 11
HE KNOWS ALL YOU KNOW 12
CHAPTER TWO
   TRUST IN LIFE 13
H2O YOU KNOW 15
I DO YOU DO WE DO 16
NEVER ALONE 17
WHEN 18
FOR YOU 19
WEAKEST PEEPS 20
FUTURE'S FUTURE 21
MERI DIEM 23
COLLECTIVELY EXHAUSTED MUTUALLY EXCLUSIVE 24
CHAPTER THREE
   DON'T GIVE ADVICE 25
ADVICE CONCISE 27
FATHER IN ME DAD I BE 28
FLOATS BOATS BACK STROKES 29
DADSTAKES & STEAKS 30
GUIDE TRIBE 31
TRAUMARAMA 32
I DON'T LIKE TO DRINK 33
WAKE EACH DAY 34
YOU ANSWERS YOU 35
LIFE CHAPTER THREE 36
CHAPTER FOUR
   THE MEEK SHALL INHERET THE EARTH 37
WHO I AM I 39
SOOO SLOW 40
FORE FOR FOUR 41
LOU'S SHOE 42
MY HO SILVER 43
EIGHT ELEVEN 44
My 45
I JUST WANNA LOVE YOU 46
AFFECTION OF CONFECTION 47
ONE SITS ALONE ON EARTH'S PERCH 48

CHAPTER FIVE
IGIT 49
B 4...51
ONE ELEVEN 52
WHERE IS JESUS TODAY..53
NO SHAME THE BLAME..54
WASTED LOVE 55
USELESS USE LESS 56
PAINFUL SUICIDE 57
NEW DIMENSION 58
ASK GOD IN AND SHARE WITH HIM 59
CHRISTMAS DAY HIS BIRTHDAY DAY 60
CHAPTER SIX
THE LEPRECHAUN..61
H.C. Berglund...63
DAYDREAMER..64
INSPECTOR RABBIT 65
WHAT ELSE GRANDPA..66
SECOND CHAIR...67
TAP THE WALL 68
ONE OF TWO...69
ANTIQUE SUITE..70
TRUFFLES SHUFFLES...71
WORD..72
CHAPTER SEVEN
ELEVEN SENSES..73
THOU SHALL NOT HAVE OTHER GODS BEFORE ME 75
THOU SHALL NOT WORSHIP ANY GRAVEN IMAGE 76
THOU SHALL NOT TAKE GODS NAME IN VAIN 77
REMEMBER THE SABBATH KEEP IT HOLY................................78
HONOR THY FATHER THY MOTHER AND THY ELDERS 79
THOU SHALL NOT MURDER..80
THOU SHALL NOT COMMIT ADULTERY 81
THOU SHALL NOT STEAL 82
THOU SHALL NOT BEAR FALSE WITNESS.................................83
THOU SHALL NOT COVET..84
LOVE THY NEIGHBOR 85
CHAPTER EIGHT
MIX OF OTHER SIX..86
HYPOCRITE...88
HELEN RED 89
BKOO BKEE...90
I'M NOT UPTIGHT..91
SHELF YOURSELF 92
MIND VISION TELEVISION...93
THRILL NOT THE KILL..94
NOT MY ALGORITHM 95
NEW SOUND FOUND 96
YOU TOO CAN TOO...97
WHAT I HOPE FOR MOST...98

                                        MY LIFE

                              FRUIT OF

APPLE OF MY EYE

                  Y

                  R

                  I

                  C

Informs of   **S**   Paraforms
My reflection lyrical poem form
Imagination Animation Information
How I perceive receive retrieve believe
I scribe describe transcribe with my tribe
The art words take shape The sum of words
Punctuation scarce Upper case after space
No extra spaces to create shapes of vases
I'm equal as the center page justification
Never on a fence Just a Happy medium
Words of few Most I knew of the few
Made up words misspelled reasons
Some mystic or cryptic Philosophic
Answers to get An internet fetch
Topics Subjects Observations
My explain Can't abstain
from writing Myrics

CHAPTER ONE
THE UNIFIER

"UNITED WE STAND

DIVIDED WE FALL"

Aesop

HONEST ABE

VERSE CURSE

LIBERTY BELL

IN MIDDLE RIDDLE

NO ONE IS WITHOUT FAULT

INDIG

BOL OF BULL

THE ADVOCATE

RELIGION DIVISION DERISION

HE KNOWS ALL YOU KNOW

HONEST ABE

Traveled and weathered
Bright smooth copper face
Sixteenth One One hundred
Obverse Graced Honesty
Each one dropped Eternity found
Red Green Brown Laying on the ground

Heads or Tails, tighten a screw
Heads or Tails, replace a fuse
Heads or Tails, bottom of wells
Heads or Tails, ALL Free as well

Sacrificed by a wicked weed
Motherly love of another
Book of Truth
Countless times read
Candlelight Bright
Land to Land
Vocabulary on his own
Knowledge negating twang
Sweet hemp pipe
Front porch heaven

Heads or Tails, tighten a screw
Heads or tails, replace a fuse
Heads or tails, bottom of wells
Heads or tails, ALL Free as well

Times of proclamations
Rivers crossed Fingers crossed
Under the cover of darkness
No engine No caboose
Lead by the bright of right
Some escape others fight
Scattered mind for Equality
Unthankful and Ungrateful
You are Welcome

VERSE CURSE

I just want to write a verse
That will cast such a curse
Where we all want to get along
And we all want to move along
Smile Wave as we pass each day

Just sing along with this song
We all get along sing along
Along we belong sing along

We all get along move along
Despite the left or the right
The wrong or the... Wrong
Where or who you've been
Give grudge a shoulder nudge
Let's do the wave of Smile Wave
Go ahead with a grin Give it a spin

Stop picking a side for this life's ride
Put the windows down Clear the air
Wave Hi to the same sky we ride by

A simple groove everyone can move
No rhythm or style Just a simple smile
A curse I can only hope gets worse
We all get along moving along
We are all in the same pot
Like it or not Smile a lot

LIBERTY BELL

The bell you hear ring
Is it your dinner to bring
or front door dinner bell
Freedom is for all to be
The liberty bell cracked
Freedom was yet a fact

Let's forge a new
To see if we are true
Let Freedom Ring
We shall Sing

Two Abrahams Freed slaves
Between them some were saved
Liberty Bell was made before the North
Told the South to shut their mouth
It cracked before they took a slap
When rung It went kung
No one sung

Let's forge a new
To see if we are true
Let Freedom Ring
God will Sing

We have all the laws to save slaves
So many written Makes some smitten
We The People enslaved ourselves
Every day Every law is broken
Round up all the guilty
We are All just filthy
slaves to the DOJ
Ding Dongs
Wrong

IN MIDDLE RIDDLE

Three you see
Is equal to me
Stuck in the middle
Equal sign Even all the time
Social mass The middle class
Between two wings Birds sing
Birds in flight Center light
Planes just the same
Trains center tracks
These are all facts

To sail with a gale
Center mass mast
Valance of balance
Even Keel Happy feel

ABC 123 Center of three
2 B even Freedom in medium
Play a fiddle The strings in middle
Sports all sorts Fiddle in the middle
Between two ears Head middle said

Moderation modulation
Rewind Pause Forward
Play Pause Equal sequel

A baby too Equal of two
Middle child Little in the middle
Sleep Work Play Divides each day
Earth's two poles The center rolls
Equilibrium A happy median
Steady Eddie Even Steven

NO ONE IS WITHOUT FAULT

Living right to be right
Does not make you right
There is a light when you're right
Day and night lead the light
Staying right can be a fight
Slight of hand will never stand

The faults in your vault
Where your warm waters halt
Feel what they feel when you are Real

When the change isn't right
or the bills stick tight
That table ain't right
Nose high in the sky
Frown some clown
From another town

The faults in your vault
Where your warm waters halt
Feel what they feel when you are Real

Your questions are your judgments
Your right Is not everyone's right
What is wrong Is you're wrong
That everyone else is wrong
He can wait to hear your
song you got wrong

INDIG

Constitutional Covenant
Simple words
In God We Trust
God Blessed America
Separation of church and state
Not separation of God and state
church and state untrustworthy
Power Greed Perversion DRENCHED

Waves of tides
Tides the waves
No beaches wade in a tidal wave
Ships will fail While innocent flail
Even at the highest trails

Who never Lied Harmed or Failed
Who is Ignored Questioned Cursed
We are His Changing it day after day
Nothing for one Everything for All
Walk in his life No gravity or wind
Light at the end Bright just right

Waves of tides
Tides the waves
No beaches wade in a tidal wave
Ships will fail While innocent flail
Even at the highest trails

Greatest NATION Covenant
keep with God His children too
Judgement day too long for some
booties to Boots Bearing the Flood
The Flood of tears The flood of spheres

BoL OF BULL

Lie able Deniable Liable
Politician starts like polit e
Ends in ician: practice Attrition
Political means lies Lies LIES
At best a salesman quest
A thesaurus hand
At a bible stand

In an outhouse
The Whitehouse
Newspaper Toiletpaper
It's worth just berthed

You took an Oath to a Covenant
Constitution Resolution Solution
Every thought that you have brought
Someone knows who you be You'll see
Thou Shall Not Bear False Witness
For an adult to lie You know what
Only worse for those Who swore to

Politician is Latin "Bearer of Lies"
Acronym BoL sounds like Bull
A Moo and a pile of Poo

Their resolute is to what fits their suit
From a suite they think they are neat
Too Political News Political Views
Hidden Truths Tries of Lies
Slacks burn concerns
Truth is fire proof

THE ADVOCATE

A new day of peace and love
Truth in the common era
Sword of equality standing free
From the deepest of wells
Born of one Raised of another
Centuries unknown Hearts the throne

I am the Air The water I Bear
What you can't see is what you need
The words you see can set you free
Lead by thee and always be free

A new day for great days
Mountain grove resting
Luck of luck Luck of lucks
Humbled father amphora full
White cloud thy brightest

I am the Air The water I Bear
What you can't see is what you need
The words you see can set you free
Lead by thee and always be free

Baseball cap crown
One for all One for All
The vocabulary of many
Already written already said
The Advocate of Truth AQUARIUS

RELIGION DIVISION DERISION

Speaking changes passing ages
Religious facts never change
Church leaders the readers
They just need to maintain
Too teach of those days
They fit these waydays
Greatness and Shame
Is always the same

People are equal
Identical in mental
Not to be told what to

Complicated perpetuated
Every religion has its division
Rules Ways Sayings and Prayings
Chants Dance Songs Gongs Wrongs
Each one unwelcoming to another
Just can't walk right in and sit within
Pass Mass Vast ceremonial task
Up and down walk around
Different days and ways

Just guide through to be true
History is our lead for all we need
Pain already done for our none

Hands high air or grasp in prayer
On your knees Sorry and Please
Bow or bow Those who know
Many fight in spite of Jesus plight
Intolerable Dishonorable Divisional
GOD is One has Ten plus One

HE KNOWS ALL YOU KNOW

Such a troubled world today
Where is the blame to display
Divisive malarky of the hierarchy
News missing trues Still a lie No deny
Social media finders by weak minders
They gave way Most immoral way for pay
Sold us out Changed our minds without a sign

Unplug to see How manipulated you be
Mind crimes Slave makers Soul breakers
It is not fair to share your flair fare or tare
Lurk Smirk Make fun of work Call out a Jerk

Conception Deception Perception
Children die Everyone cries
Find the underlies No tries
There was this dad by me
Murdered his babies of three
What drives a dad to go mad
Innocent pure always ignored
Their murder rate a heart rate
Parking lots Tot lots Minds rot
Datalogic psychologic pathologic
Never have we seen before Implore

Unplug to see How manipulated you be
Mind crimes Slave makers Soul breakers
It is not fair to share your flair fare or tare
Lurk Smirk Make fun of work Call out a Jerk

Acronyms of the Ment Meant what they bent
The crime is You gave it all away Without a say
Everyday a piece of you For them too play
Race baiters Gender benders Gas lighters
Used against you every wayday for pay
Delete feeds for Dinner table needs
Free space is the home space
Face to Face Grace in place
Smiles spread for miles
Just for fun do a Trial run

12

CHAPTER TWO

TRUST IN LIFE

Trust life is such
Such a life to trust
Hope is for the pope
Believe in you get
What you put in
Especially when
Not for you

H2O YOU KNOW

I DO YOU DO WE DO

NEVER ALONE

WHEN

FOR YOU

WEAKEST PEEPS

FUTURE'S FUTURE

PAUSE EQUALITY

MERI DIEM

COLLECTIVELY EXHAUSTED

MUTUALLY EXCLUSIVE

H2O YOU KNOW

Start life afloat Not in a boat
Nine months in a water sack
We grow From In and Of H2O
Seventy percent of precipitant
Hydro of another generation
Breathe it in Breathe it out
Drink it in Sweat it out

Mix Stir Swirl Squirt
Frost   Boil
Soak   It   Wet
Blow   Dry
Say Don't spray

Can't live in it But must have in it
The air has a lot of water to bear
Hangs around above ground
Rain drops The snow falls
It bubbles and troubles
Bye tides Waves bye
Steam or a stream
Flows and slows
Cloudy clear
Its always
Here

Swish Spit
Wash   Rinse
Color   Filter
Suspend Upend

Sea level Knee level
Canada floats a boats
Slim Jim Swims in gym
Don't forget slippery when wet
China bowls and toilet bowls
Swirls around flushes down
The solution to pollution
Shall never be Dilution

I DO YOU DO WE DO

Make your love a bad habit
They are hardest to break
Put each other first Tie in life
Best friends to the bitter end
Grow everyday Learn everyday

One
Family dinner
I do You do We do
He said She said We said
Her side His side Our side
One bread
Winner

Animosity
begins with pain
It grows and shows
while no one knows
Never a reason to be sorry
Live by action Not by words
No shame No pain Play in the rain

One
Breadwinner
I do You do We do
He said She said We said
Her side His side Our side
One Family
dinner

Last one out Fluffs it out
The bed you make your own
The flaws You need to love them All
If you were grinning in the beginning
The ending shall never be pending

NEVER ALONE

Forget everything you want
You are everything they need
Your lead is Their way is your way

Innocence lost Innocence found
Child no more Insomnia more
Love to work to love
Feelings senses Love Intuition
No tuition for intuition
Faithful Tearful supplications

Forget everything you want
You are everything they need
Your lead is Their way is your way

Your past guides their future
Attention fewest wise words
Terrible parent Best parent
Both good bad and a choice
Friendship and love ends each day
Each has to make their own way

Forget everything you want
You are everything they need
Your lead is their way is your way

WHEN

When you were born an innocent form
A perfect ten in the buff Looking ruffed
A new world When eyes open wide
Future bright When kept right
Beauty in the eyes When

When a toddler a little waddler
Never a seat with moving feet
Chitter chatter and Pitter patter
Memories fade like a vague dream
When some memories were dreams
Wires get crossed information tossed

When almost a teen Nature gets mean
Puberty storm Weather together When
awkward gawky sulky bulky senses When
It will fade When age to another page

When eighteen the world gets mean
Adults maybe Mostly the legal sense
Few cents or common sense When
No guide When the parents' cents
makes no sense in the past tense
Common sense your cents When

When you know what bestowed
When you see the beauty two make be
When you believe Get what you need
When you learn too teach too Learn
When to say When to know When

FOR YOU

When we are born No matter shape or form
There's a purpose in life Just like a bug's life
Everything matters even when in tatters
What we see Only scratches the surface
of every creature's actual purpose
We are first at being the worst

Everyone before you It took two
A piece of each Is you
FOR YOU
To make your way
Better than they

Parents is two
Grandparents is four
Great grandparent's eight
And Sixteen more before
A lot of ways to find your way
Reader Writer Singer or a Ringer
A shortened graph for your life path
Find what they knew or they could do
As simple as that for you to unpack
Basic facts will get you on track

Everyone before you It took two
A piece of them Is you
FOR YOU
To make your way
Better than they

Old names Surnames Their names just the same
Tells the past really fast Don't let this get passed
Those days they had their ways as today
Just listen to what you been missing
Hindsight will always be right
Your past is your pass
For your clearest path

19

WEAKEST PEEPS

Humans are the weakest
On foot nowhere to put
Into the wilderness they go
Prepared as they know
End in this way

How long can you
Sit before you quit
In the pouring rain
Snow falls covers all
Night calls Sun falls

Some make it a day
Each passing day
Another passing away
Unprepared just unaware
People are the weakest

Bears don't have a care
They fair in dens they prepare
Birds Squirrels Rabbits Deer
Have no gear for their fear
They freely roam their home
Outdoor Rain Sleet Snow

Top of the food chain
We think we know it all
Bikes and cars get us far
Heating homes Ringing phones
Endless water flow and drains go
Still can't make it a day Nature's way

FUTURE'S FUTURE

I don't know what the future holds
I know how I need to conduct myself
For me to see the future of me
My immunity is of the day before
Ask me tomorrow about today

Crystal balls roll and fall
The heck with Tarot deck
Palm read not to agree

Our future is not of our choosing
We will do everything to change
what we think the future to be
The better way for each day
Start each with love of each

When you refrain
Your brain unrestrained
Pretend is a Best friend

Love everything you see
For the happier you will be
Love When What How you do
Will always make A Happy You too
Days without frays Plays Happy Days
The future I see you are Happy to be

< = >

Fast forward, Rewind
Song in between
Harmony of two
Different sounds the same
Right ear Left ear
Frequency absorbed
Echoes in the folds

Press pause for life
Press pause for equality
Press pause for love
Press pause for peace

Equality is Three
Double-edge sword
End to End
Heads and Tails
Places Faces Colors
Equality remains same
A happy medium

Press pause for life
Press pause for equality
Press pause for love
Press pause for peace

Less than poor
Greater than rich
Misery at each end
Staring across the equal sign
Truth does lie Equaled by Honesty
Pause for Equality to be One

MERI DIEM

Clocks tick tock
Watches just click
Rewind to stay on
Time ticks by bye

Sun dial to plug in
Batteries last not fast
Crystals click seconds split
Two plates of Pi divided by
Arms called hands that point

New days raise with rays
Time never stops never ends
A shift of light into night

Keeping time for a time
Hourglass an equal pass
From a turn An hour to burn
Two hours pass to return the turn
Interrupt The time gives up
Grains refrain a funnel tunnel
Wasting time to keep time

Twenty-four per diem
More than four we snore
Sixteen to make serene

Meridiem line keeps the time
Ante up the sun comes up
Start another day of way
After moon before noon
End the day grateful way
Post noon before moon

COLLECTIVELY EXHAUSTED MUTUALLY EXCLUSIVE

Now you went and messed up
Now everyone is dressed up
I was always there But you didn't really care
When you don't care You really won't fare
It was your flair is why I wasn't there
O'You care when you start to see the flare

You know that I know all that you know
Day night Spite right Contrite polite
See me Tery In the C.E.M.E.Tery
Oh the contrary See me Tery

Two gates in Only one can see
Chain link gates to the pearly gates
Ten was hard Now eleven is even harder
That's what happens when you get smarter
Blood Sweat and fears Apologetical tears
Welcome home to our home

You know that I know all that you know
Day night Spite right Contrite polite
See me Tery In the C.E.M.E.Tery
Oh the contrary See Me Tery

Plots, plaques and spired stones
Prayers Dates and those pearly gates
Thoughtful steps Facing stones
Some names known Mostly unknown
Space is a waste Imagination faith
Tears hello Let them flow

CHAPTER THREE

DON'T GIVE ADVICE

Give experience
Ample examples
Truth with proof
Reciprocate
Learning trait

ADVICE CONCISE

FATHER IN ME DAD I BE

FLOATS BOAT BACK STROKES

DADSTAKES & STEAKS

GUIDE TRIBE

TRAUMARAMA

I DON'T LIKE TO DRINK

WAKE EACH DAY

YOU ANSWERS YOU

LIFE CHAPTER THREE

ADVICE CONCISE

Growing up I ran amuck
Nine skateboards Never paid for
Snowballs throw cars to and fro
Swats at school a mosquito count
I wasn't a rookie at playing hooky
Not a prankster or a gangster

My advice concise precise
Don't let Want feed your Need
Find a comfortable pace
For your life race

Paper routes Grass gets stout
Brothers clothes didn't fit so well
Pants in a bunch under belts scrunch
Loved to work for pants that work
Face to Face you see my grace
Sun-weathered son Granddad one

For your life race
Find a comfortable pace
Don't let Want feed your Need
My advice concise precise

I lead my three Twenty-five years each
75 years of kids ways through life's maze
Taller Stronger Smarter and easy to see
Each better I see Each chapter of me
At forty-four I was still immature
Not sixty yet and still not yet

FATHER IN ME DAD I BE

How it became to be
The father I have become
The dad I never got to see
Two on paper a spare in air
The example of my Grandpa
Was the best of the rest
Polarity right polite
Opposite ample
of examples

Me Myself and I gave it a try
Much of my dismay to say
Female cracks
Straighten the tracks

Neither was I perfect at
As a son I was a squirrely one
As a dad not bad But surely one
I fixed most of what my kids twist
Waste no way fix for another day
Someone else's hands Mine too
No need to fight Just be right
Learn too follow too lead

Me Myself and I gave it a try
Much of my dismay to say
Female cracks
Straighten the tracks

My one regret that I fret
My father deserving most
I still have yet to have met
Biological met Adult not yet
How did I be the elder never seen
Just believe He is there with care
Imagine the dad you need the most
It is not a fantasy your children you see
God blessed you Now you bless them

FLOATS BOATS BACK STROKES

I'm sorry the times I realized
What I knew was never new to you
I tried much to teach you so much
There is a feeling you will know
That will bring you to a slow
The event may not be the same
Doesn't change the feeling of shame

There is one day for you to say
But every day father's day
Is a different way with no say

I threw you from a boat
Yanked you by a rope
Grandma's pool acted a fool
My schools had swimming pools
Whip kick Scissors kick Float trick
Like a monkey at the zoo
I don't quite sink like you

There is one day for you to say
But every day father's day
Is a different way with no say

We live this way together I say
The father I be I never got to see
Yet the path was right to be polite
A stronger one on a higher rung
Chapter two is in front of you
Chapter three is where I see
Shoes don't care how you wear
Wear them out to be stout
Use your brains to move trains

DADSTAKES & STEAKS

Learn today Learn tomorrow
Forever more Learn some more
Friend or foe as long as you know
Do today Twice as hard another day
Don't give advice Give experience
Never strike the female like

Health is our wealth
Wealth kills our health
only this One body of fun

Instinct way more than you think
There's no scribe when baby arrives
Manual for one No fun for another one
Just no way to know They show and grow
The more you lie The harder you have to try
The trouble becomes more than double
Admit your mistake correct your mistake
Right is learned in simplest terms

Moderation of everything
Or lose the fun parts of you
Steps and reps keeps you pep

Mashed potatoes No way at the buffet
To cook Looks good Smells good It's good
Eye contact with crosser by in a drink line
Green light you For a flood to pass thru
Bitter Sweet Salt Meat Your body knows
The stomach has The glutton button

GUIDE TRIBE

There was a bubble you can't see
My bubble space of your safe space
Trouble you made sort of your way
I let you be so I could see for me
The men you would see to be
I'm sorry to say that I may
have got in your way
in so many ways

The line you never crossed
My outer bubble of trouble
Was just by luck big enough
Your mom kept the leashes
At times they were too tight
No matter the stink that you think
Our home school was pretty cool
As we graduate with our traits
Our history is not a mystery
We learn every turn
There is a tribe
Our guide
There is a tribe
We learn at every turn
Our history is not a mystery
As we graduate with our traits
Our home school was pretty cool
No matter the stink that you think
At times they were too tight
Your mom kept the leashes
Was just by luck big enough
My outer bubble of trouble
The line you never crossed

Your bubbles grew for your kids too
I've let mine drop without a pop
My bubble air is now your spare
Your leaks fix from your inside
Fix today for tomorrow days
My spare is just for stare
The tribe scribes inside

31

TRAUMARAMA

What am I to say
Ways of my childhood
A pain they complained
I can explain my complain
No blindfold just mindful
All I said I would never do
Be more than I knew
I thought I knew it all
So how could I fall

Clear Domesphere
Heart doesn't part
Deep sound sleep

Try as I might
There is some spite
It comes down to this
A tale to pass down trail
Can't win them all in thrall
Differential inferential parental

Lessons learned it's your turn
All you said would never do
Only need to do is be true

There will be a day of say
Offsprings point of your way
They'll shed light of your plight
My plight is to shed some light
Parents learn while teaching stern
Mistakes Struggle Strife Makes right
Stronger ones on higher rungs

I DON'T LIKE TO DRINK

Not for reasons you think
My life Mostly drank Highlife
Beer for me never ends at three
Rum is fun but it makes me dumb
Every mistake outtake and break
Shameover always takes over
Feeling guilt under a quilt
So much to do after too
Way before two

Cheers with beers
Shots no way Life the next day
Covenant think before you drink

Feeling that way Waste another day
Never let my children Feel my for real
My father called my dad a drunk
Loser boozer instead of me he said
Scared me to think If I did drink
Almost a man I met the man
Handed a beer
Told me to steer
Inappropriate as it gets
I was young drinking was fun
Foamy heads Life comes to ahead
Sober life No strife on body or life
Emotional drink Makes worse reverse
Addiction is self-infliction Slave of sort
There is a time and place Slow pace

Dangly back of throat Size of boat
Flung over Slun gover Fun sover
Hungoverslept feeling unkept

Lives lost a few putting back a few
Hendrix Joplin Denver Names a few
In true Billions of names are gone too
Ill health No wealth Family mental health
Thousands of years since the first drink
Death and destruction We still Drink

WAKE EACH DAY

Thank God in YOUR own way
For your new day to play and pay
Without a word to say or pray ANY way
No bible No Church Nor a cross on a perch
End each day grateful for your EVERY way
If your day is not going your way
Turn back for the right of way

Want some Buy some Get some
Know some Borrow some Pocket some
Eat some Drink some Smoke some

Write down what you got
Whether you still like it or not
Stop depreciating what you appreciated
Confounded what you compounded
Enough is more than enough
So much storage and stuff

Want some Buy some Get some
Know some Borrow some Pocket some
Eat some Drink some Smoke some

When will it ever end
The need for power and speed
Water and feed Is all we really need
Don't join the crowd Watch a cloud
Your purchases not your purposes
Another song all we got wrong
Sing along and let me write
the song we get right

YOU ANSWERS YOU

Inside of you is you
Thinking without speaking
Talking in your head instead
You knows all you Do Done Did
Everyone talks to and answers too
What if you Is someone else
The never disrespect one

For a day I spent this way
My Grandpa me inside me
Memory sound of his voice
To everything I said or did
Didn't stop in my tracks
Had a few pause because
I knew he disapproved

A great day with He as me
I confide I had to apologize
Just for fun did another one
His say never an ill way
My respect for him
Steep and Deep

After a week reality speak
My version A better person
Apologies of my past came fast
I have a cast of others past
God as my father the easiest
He only has eleven rules
I promise you will make you
A better you to answer to

LIFE CHAPTER THREE

I am sorry not sorry
for the fun things in life
That weren't exactly right
A fast drive Big pride Big ride
A gramps I be My immaturity I see
Wish I knew the true influence on you
No one ever told me What I now see

I love you more
Than you will ever know
Things I've said Things I've done
Remains unknown when you're grown

Maybe someone told me
No retention of the mentioned
At twenty-five my first came alive
At fifty I see my first grandbaby of me
I still have a role Not the one at my waist
Twenty-five years of extra fight mostly right

I love you more
Than you will ever know
Things I've said Things I've done
Remain unknown when you're grown

Like the mirror on the passenger door
The reflection you see I am closer than I be
Sometimes slight makes things right
I made you rough and tough
But sensitive too stuff
Sleek and Meek
Me I See

CHAPTER FOUR

THE MEEK SHALL
INHERET THE EARTH

Seeks climbing peaks
Reserve Preserve Conserve
No know better than though
offensive not Offensive
Conceive reprieve
from believe

WHO I AM I

SOOO SLOW

FORE FOR FOUR

LOU'S SHOE

MY HO SILVER

EIGHT ELEVEN

MY POINT

I JUST WANNA LOVE YOU

AFFECTION OF CONFECTION

ONE SITS ALONE ON EARTH'S PERCH

WHO I AM I

I was born a baby boy
Soiled and toiled
I grew into a man
Is how I stand
I am a carpenter
A tin banger
A jack of all

Who I am I
I am what I seek
Is to be Meek
Inherit the Earth
Without a perch
in front of a church

I am a good neighbor
I am a brother and of another
I am a dad a father a grandfather
I am a friend an acquaintance
I am at best a guest of the rest
I am a family man a happy fan

Who I am I
I am what I seek
Is to be Meek
Inherit the Earth
Without a perch
in front of a church

I am a reacher a teacher
I am a searcher a researcher
I am a learner a steady earner
I am a hunter a fisher a sower
I am not religious God my father
I am what I seek is to be meek

SOOO SLOW

Gotta go Gotta go
You're driving so slow
I need to get by
Signal Clicker Flasher
Driving faster Blow on by
Your doors goodbye
Sayonara Bye Bye

Gotta go Gotta go
My get up and go Gotta go
Gotta go I got up and went

Heavy pedal not to metal
I ain't asking you to speed
Just do the speed limit
Git r dun on the left
Center we all get along
Slow and the might
Stay on the right

Gotta go Gotta go
My get up and go Gotta go
Gotta go I got up and went
See ya don't wanna be ya

No stare don't care
Slower than my gator
After while crocodile
Everyone has their space
No race car or pace car
Your slow pace has a place
Right of me where I see
Sayonara blowin by Bye

FORE FOR FOUR

Cheer up When Tee up
Tee time or when free time
Fair weather days to play
Damp days cart pathways
Snow days No ways

Bogus Bogey Fogy
Slice plays in ways
Regal is the Eagle

Off tract First shwack
Son of a gun A Mulligan
Green seen a fair way away
Fairway wood Hybrid could
Ball didn't drop on
Have to chip on

Hazards Traps
Trees Leaves three
Cart path launch
Hotdog lunch

Putt Putt Pro
But the preen green
Home free with three
Cat with a cotton ball
Flagpole hole avoidable
Mutter utter with putter
Pissed Divot fix and a six

LOU'S SHOE

A spider was a little hider
It was certain the window curtain
Like Lou would hide from view
Crawled overhead Above the bed
Not in the mood to be rude
Please just move along
and we'll get along

Skin crawls
When spiders fall
Spiders we meet
We may eat
when we sleep

The news is over
I want to turn over
You're still there with a stare
A shoe and you'd be through
A mess at best But if I miss
Spider falls for my flaw
Yell that he had fell
Couch my pillow bed

Fiddle on the back
In your nap sack
A bite that might
turn your skin black

How about toilet tissue
A different kind of a shew
To rid Fred above my head
One of a hundred Litter leader
Mosquito eater No web cleaner
Out the window Fred said
He left his family's bed
Fred or Lou's New
Above my bed

MY HO SILVER

She's a long tall Sally Barely fit an alley
Pretty in the face Wide in the base
Whole lot a yank from a diesel tank
Big silver truck Sits four and up
Hwistling Ho Turbo blows
Dream truck can't get stuck

Back in the day A carpenter I say
A truck I need Nor could I afford
Now I have a truck Just hauls my butt

Just my luck to a ford that truck
My business success not of the rest
Luxury ride Touring our countryside
Shore to shore She drove many more
Rocky Mtns Smooth thru the grooves
Yellow Stone made some yellow snow
Slept in the bed by some riverbeds

Back in the day A carpenter I say
A truck I need Nor could I afford
Now I have a truck Just hauls my butt

It's a rich man's truck That I am not
It makes me sad to see guys like me
Fender flapper trucks stuck in ruts
I hear some say I like your truck
Makes me feel like I suck
Owning such a truck

EIGHT ELEVEN

It is not for me to say
To believe a word I say
I have lived a lot of ways
This art splays my heart
Truth days of my ways
Each line that I write
a discussion of mine
A tear in my eye
For my Belief
His Relief

How do you rate up to eight
We circulate the infinity eight
Eleven it takes for one circulate
Three it may take or incinerate

Everyone knows the Ten of those
One more of those not a propose
Thee atoning son
Father One
Love everyone
as I have loved you

How do you rate up to eight
We circulate the infinity eight
Eleven it takes for one circulate
Three it may take or incinerate

There is three to rub all over
Trust me It is like poison ivy
Eight you can't break
SHALL is not a pal
Thee of Three
Prorate of
Other
Eight

My

disability
Dis my ability
So how can it be
These words of an art
That flow without a chart
Stigma Enigma Name on a box
A daydreamer I may be
Imagination Animation
Is why I think outside the box

Go kick rocks with your box of rocks
Thought for myself I taught myself
Clicker channel mixer problem fixer
Learn to teach Not what to teach

An end A always head of the class
Lucky if I got a pass at the end of class
I can spell as you can tell Not with math
Two plus two equals four I implore
Social studies made some sense
Our vocabulary is full of crap
Gym an A all thru my days

Go kick rocks with your box of rocks
Thought for myself I taught myself
Clicker channel mixer problem fixer
Learn to teach not what to teach

My enigma is I'm a sigma
An elephant mind playing rewind
No disability just responsibility
To find the opposite ability
You should always see
A purpose that be
Extra words to
end the
Point

I JUST WANNA LOVE YOU

Our life mars and scars
Reform what is torn
We have come so far
Try to stay who we are

I JUST WANNA LOVE YOU
Lose spite never fight
A Mulligan to love again
Easy to say Locked hard away
A hard fight to love right

I JUST WANNA LOVE YOU
Our life luggage has to be checked
To carry on would be to carry on
The baggage is old and worn
We need to throw away
To be on our merry way

I JUST WANNA LOVE YOU
How we are here Right now
Content in our content
Unfurled our world
Free of the past
For us to last

I JUST WANNA LOVE YOU
Snuggle up Cuddle up
When afar under stars
Home base each face
You tell me to sit up
So I get up and we go
To the stars past Mars

AFFECTION OF CONFECTION

The fame of Sugarcane
The pharos had marshmallows
A sweet treat Still neat to eat
A sugar high A slice of pie
Rockets Glue Candy too
Crystal Powder Brown

Taffy pulls and folds
Sour Tart Cut apart
Saltwater chew

Sugar beets Has these beat
Sugarcane doesn't grow the same
Sweet corn High fructose born
Molasses not of the masses
The fakes have no stake

Cupcakes Coffee cakes
Layer cakes Pound cakes
Square Round Upside down

My other girls with swirls
My affection of confection
Convection baked oven cakes
Little Debbie with confetti
A gem is Dolly Madison
Prancer dancer Krispy Kreme
Reign supreme Some with cream

ONE SITS ALONE ON EARTH'S PERCH

Day so cold Snow so bold
Layering on your back
Natures camo sack
Waiting on a rack
Shivered tired Take a nap
Snap awake A twig did break
Eye spy something brown in my eye
A doctor's take for a piece of steak
Hold still This may sting a little

To teach the family tree
The meat is better for thee
Nature's way a better day

Public land is where I stand
On a rare I've missed by a hair
Matrix buck had more than luck
Jumped the string at a stream
He ran that day blowing away
Found my arrow towards the lake
His gait made my arrow break
Never broke an arrow like this
I was sure I wouldn't miss

To teach the family tree
The meat is better for thee
Nature's way a better day

How raw is it to say
My hands thaw in this way
The love of Pete its meat to eat
Morbid to say but truth anyway
Sorry first before cut off the purse
No point Cut straight up the gut
No one likes meat with a stink
Cut the windpipe arm so warm
Entrails away Asphalt trail far away
Another way to say it nature's way
Grateful Graceful Tasteful Bellyful

CHAPTER FIVE

IGIT

IGIT is Legit
IGIT In Deo Speravi
IGIT In God I Trust
IGIT Is all we need
IGIT We need to believe
IGIT A new day Everyday

B4

ONE ELEVEN

WHERE IS JESUS TODAY

NO SHAME THE BLAME

WASTED LOVE

USELESS USE LESS

PAINFUL SUICIDE

NEW DIMENSION

ASK GOD IN SHARE WITH HIM

CHRISTMAS DAY HIS BIRTHDAY DAY

B 4

Imagine any man today
In the days of Jesus ways
Some sorted stories of sin
scribed same book as him
Sins brought before him
In a tent and at a well

Look in the mirror too
Jesus' heart Is part of you
Yourself Himself is You

Blasphemy bellows loud
Hear me out Voice no clout
Imagine a gene pool his tool
Some say two of Mary's too
So that makes four for sure
What if I say is true today

Look in the mirror too
Jesus' heart Is part of you
Yourself Himself is You

Throw the yellow flag
For a man to say No
When the girls say hello
Instinctive distinctive reactive
Man's state is to procreate
Woman's desire sets the fire
Yesterday's ways Just as today's

ONE ELEVEN

One really third Prior was two
Ten already carved Said Ignored
Eleventh said Scribed Ignored
One more command for thee

Thy love thee thou hath love thy
To be free Love thee It is always free
Always love thee Not for me

He came to That was his own
30 years grown 3 years a roam
In the beginning was the Word
Life the light the world did not know
Grace placed in Grace of Grace

Thy love thee thou hath loved thy
To be free Love thee It is always free
Always love Thee Not for me

Helping hands from empty hands
Son Brother Father Brother of another
Shallow wading cousin blessed
Town days to town Feet on the ground
Water and rest to teach the rest

WHERE IS JESUS TODAY

Signs at churches On perches
Telephone poles as roads roll
He has come He has risen
Life to cheer or live in fear
What does Would he look like
No way the Virgin Mary way
What would his arrive derive

Spend a day and ponder way
No magic poof in God's proof
World impure for Innocent Pure

How in the world if your world
Look around our world today
Where would you start
Who would you trust
The world ignores God
Don't expect to get a nod
My guess It will be a mess
Come right in Be killed for sin

Spend a day and ponder way
No magic poof with God's proof
World impure for Innocent Pure

We are so immune to deception
Has misconception caused
us to miss his reception
There is those Who hide UFOs
Powers be Belittle Betray Display
Most just dismiss as craziness
Is he the one coming back
or someone from outback
Jesus told disciples old
Advocate of truth
Will have proof

NO SHAME THE BLAME

Merry Contrary
A blush is not a rush
You feel when you wrong
Your sign you're not fine
The fine is your tuition
Should have used intuition
Leads away from institutions

Shame for blame
No shame the blame
If shame is lame
You are too Blame

Innocent lost Method the blame
Ignorance the reason blame is lame
Laziness make laws Always of flaws
Family Morals Common sense
Less born less die relativity costs

Shame for blame
No shame the blame
If shame is lame
You are too Blame

So many laws being born is illegal
Life of crime freedom not Free
Power and greed is the feed
Laws forgotten unknown once signed
Shame is the crime and punishment
A family mistaken Elders forsaken

WASTED LOVE

I love to
peddle away
Through my days
I love my new bicycle
Peddle brakes comfy seat
But there is a new bike
Comfy seat peddle brakes
I want this new bicycle

Wheels go round
Appreciation falls down
Gratitude is your latitude
Disposable is unreasonable

My bicycle isn't the same
It gets me where need be
It is shiny Stops on a dime
Up a hill Around a bend
Back around home again
It's everything I need

Wheels go round
Appreciation falls down
Gratitude is your latitude
Disposable is unreasonable

The new bicycle is shinier
Tire teats a different seat
I don't love my bicycle
Just like the new one
Not a scratch Not a squeak
Not even a tear in the seat
Love forgotten after a week

USELESS USE LESS

Less is the gist not a jest
Less is the lesson of less
Less is much less a mess
Less mess not a guess
Less trash to stash
Less stash of trash

Less pollution in the air is fair
LESS IS THE SOLUTION TO POLLUTION
Less solutions that is pollution
Less to pollute is resolute

Less of want to confront
Less need to work is a perk
Less bills to pay more time to play
Less boulders upon your shoulders
Less depressed when not pressed

Less lessens this lesson
Less stress about this mess
Less should impress the rest
Less distress on life's quest
Less tense a happy sense
Less is more for sure
Less is just the best
Less is a gist list

Less Hopelessness
Less sorrow for tomorrow
Less spending no pending
Less content to be content
Less sad to make mad
Less wear and tear
Less fare for flair
Less at best
Is just less

PAINFUL SUICIDE

Impossible to understand What is at hand
A feeling sense of no sense of presence
Pain gained retained No refrain
Less of worth No worth or from birth
Life is tough enough So rough
An easy way out no doubt

Your sun Your sky Your clouds
Your rain Your snow Yourself
Your shadow over a shallow
Your love of you to push thru

The mess left for the rest
A picture scene never unseen
By the ones that cared the most
You're the culprit They're suspects
Police and fire in their attire
Make fun of you while bagging you
The coroner too Your carcass of you
Because of you Their memory too

Your sun Your sky Your clouds
Your rain Your snow Yourself
Your shadow over a shallow
Your love of you to push thru

No commandment said you can't
But to present with malintent
a particular way you will pay
Your everyday God's purpose way
Imagination belief relief no grief
It is free for you to see Believe me
No magical poof Time brings proof

NEW DIMENSION

Old days
The fifth dimension
Dawned Age of Aquarius
From a booming generation
Peace and love rarely seen
The biggest star Brightest star
Aquarius born another name
Elders working of their own
A child's compass spins
Direction and path
unknown

A new day the sun shined in
Quenched and Drenched
Air with care Water too bear
Aquarius Aquarius Aquarius

A tent of two Two at a well
Spare a stone Hide the throne
Living water thirst no more
Water living forever more
Across a sea Over an ocean
Meek timekeepers ire

A new day the sun shined in
Quenched and Drenched
Air with care Water too bear
Aquarius Aquarius Aquarius

Fifty-Seven years grown
Three years to roam
A thirty-year career
Future Elder of Eternity
Intelligent evolution in life
Day dreamer mild demeanor
Always following sense of right
A humbled father graced by His

58

ASK GOD IN AND SHARE WITH HIM

Here's the deal God is real
You cannot see But you can feel
His presence in you before you
Look at a reflection of your face
You're his child You look like him
He will always be there in you
You must take care of you
and those born of you

See something you love
Ask God in and share with him
Doing something you love
Ask God in and share with him

Religious scholars give a holler
But I don't care for their flair
I'll never be as religious as thee
What I believe is what I know
Who I know is who I feel
God is a big deal For real

Being with those who you love
Ask God in and share with him
Find beauty in what surrounds you
Ask God in and share with him

When I ride my motorcycle
I ask my Grandpa to ride inside
Two of my friends are gone
There are songs that play
We jam inside out No doubt
Air guitar afar Snare in the air
Ask God to He jams too
We wrote this song for you

CHRISTMAS DAY HIS BIRTHDAY DAY

Santa Claus children believe
Free falls the flue Toys for you
Which brings many questions to you
The sleigh to say seems far-fetched
Older siblings say Aw no way
Kids at school are talking too

A surprise disguise of God's sort
Take pause for this Santa's clause
Day night Spite right Contrite polite
You know He knows ALL that you know

He they cannot see Though for you to show
You too can believe in what you cannot see
Transition Santa's story into God's Glory
What you are blessed by your success
Should be less of a Christmas mess

A surprise disguise of God's sort
Take pause for this Santa's clause
Day night Spite right Contrite polite
You know He knows ALL that you know

Believing what you cannot see
Reprieve from make-believe
Christmas Eve
Promise the Lord Innocence awards
For the next day Gifts on display
Christmas day His Birthday day
His worth far beyond his birth
Jesus seen The manger scene

CHAPTER SIX

THE LEPRECHAUN

Just a little primer
I'm yet an old-timer
Reasonably seasoned
Many reasons Many seasons
Life is such of much
Is what is is

H C BERGLUND

DAYDREAMER

INSPECTOR RABBIT

WHAT ELSE GRANDPA

SECOND CHAIR

TAP THE WALL

ONE OF TWO

ANTIQUE SUITE

TRUFFLES SHUFFLES

WORD

H.C. Berglund

Protected undetected
He is the saint that I ain't
Innocent and Innocence
Inside me the best of me
Good Samaritan nursery picture
Newspaper page of that day
Certificate of Birth Not on earth
Changed at two Known by a few
For selfishness and immaturity
Thrown away with no say
Never told why
Hidden deep inside
Pure from impure world
Protected from the erected
Safe and sound until I found
At a stop area
A Bearer of Christ
In a Mountain Grove
Observing our every day
A poet who didn't know
A writer with a typewriter
Without any words to say
Words of few written true
Names of six
One letter C is me
Letter number three
Four names not the same

DAYDREAMER

When I was small in every class
There was always a wall of glass
Trees Grass Some cool cars pass
Many like me Dream days away
A flaw A stigma A scarlet letter
Teachers thought they were taught
I'm just a Daydreamer What do I know
Wasn't slow Wasn't a pro They didn't know

It was a name that carried shame
The blame was not so much the name
They could not teach I did not know
How was I to discern from a stern
It is not so much what was read
But how it would swirl in my head
They showed me math Science too
Teaching was too much reaching
So from my chair A glassy stare
Always in trouble until I grew stubbles

Walking home like I lived in roam
Twelve blocks away the postal way
Rain sleet and snow This I know
Scores of Chores Grounded Confounded
The concern from the stern didn't learn
Too much to do than learn with you
One rule for me to rate Was to graduate
Rule fulfilled but the rage of this page
I wasn't in the parade across the stage
Diploma loading dock on a different clock
One final punch from a school of fools

INSPECTOR RABBIT

His name was You you see
Wires and pliers Is all you need
Install a ceiling fan She said please
The wires three You could leave be
Missing wire cap Tape that tap
Fan said Hi The wires didn't fry
Makes a happy guy in her eye
Wrong still plays a good song
It is still a note that I wrote
Now your shocked
Because I rock

I spend my days where rabbits stay
Going thru spaces of other people's places
Hoping not to see Any kind of faces

Loose wires Retired wires Live wires
Pressed paper glue Foam other goo
Outside wood Used to be wood
Asbestos lead water and paint
Radon gas Realtors asks
Rain stains water drains
One concrete kind that cracks
Big long cracks in the mortar gaps
Concrete blocks unsound when round

I work my role in rabbit holes
Every domicile is on trial
I compare to keep it fair

Everyone is an electrician
No matter how wrong you do
and if you survive wires alive
Flip of a switch without a twitch
Light fixture works while you twerk
Not trying to be a jerk It's just my work
We are loved and hated Reports paraded
Many sorts of a Home Inspector's reports

WHAT ELSE GRANDPA

How in the world did I end up
In such a puddle of girl trouble
Proud to see my grandbabies of me
Three boys of mine No girlie kind
Brought daughters into life's party
To bring so cute into the boys' club

How dare the three of you
So many boys Eyes of blue
some other eye colors too
How dare the three of you

My for real of this deal
That melts my heart of stone
These little girls Swirls of Curls
Little dresses and hair messes
Their sweet little voices Shew

WHAT ELSE YOU WANNA
TALK ABOUT GRANDPA

How dare the three of you
Make me feel this way each day
Glassy eyes Occasional sniffle
How dare the three of you

What am I to do with such a reach
Granddaughter each is just a peach
Mom's Hair bows and color toes
Heals High squeals Shopping deals
It's just so much cute to compute
I'm just a mess in a puddle of yes
A tired mess in a puddle of yes
Blessed in a puddle of mess

SECOND CHAIR

Always be
The Better Person
Know your truth
Then walk away
Never a word to say
Let ignorance have its way
It will learn another wayday

No one can ever do
Because nothing can ever
be about only you

To always find kind
Everyone else gets their way
Be little Sit in the middle
Looming unassuming
Always there with care
No person ever there
with a spare

No one can ever do
Because nothing can ever
Be about only you

Ghosting is vocabulary for
attention seeking opinion
To shame common sense
thinking when things
are better left unsaid
Mirror way about your day
No sense hosting a roasting

TAP THE WALL

Long stride I glide
A gait that can jump gates
Never a race Just a fast pace
From a small town No ride around
Walked everyday met some halfway
To schools and to pools
Peds wearing keds

Called a mall walker
My long stride a fast ride
Doesn't hurt my pride

Small city Center of city
Loitering crowd not allowed
Our small mall Shops an all
Street like maze No rainy days
Hang out when school drains out
Other malls with tall walls
Open space to pace

Life's ride kids stride
Courting at Food courts
Flat bill hats Giant shoe racks
A whole lot of proof of youth

Mornings start with older hearts
Mall walkers Bench talkers Gawkers
Meanders Ganders with Candor
Reps of steps some with pep
Tap the wall try not to fall
Malls falling their walls

ONE OF TWO

Water bearers eyes of blue
One of two younger than two
Two years Booties of bronze
A storm grows Shingles blown
Truck of cars driven away
A new roof A new father
Across town Families frown
Few more towns to settle down
Two fathers unknown watching alone

One of Two Younger of Two
Story untold already unfold
Older of four Not sure if more

A child grown One father known
Both sit alone for reasons known
Irish twins Aquarian twin Jr's junior
Dad Pops Licorice drops
Beers Cheers Sheet metal shears
New sisters two In the middle too

One of Two Younger of Two
Story untold already unfold
Older of four Not sure if more

Callused hands pictures of pride
Thin as a rail as a fence is high
Plaque-less walls intelligence full
Best education self-education
Looks and smarts of Honest Abe
Honesty ample by his example

ANTIQUE SUITE

When I was small an all
My grandparents built a room
For my great-grandparents
Granny and Pa He was tall
Memory faint in a fog

Queen B and these
Granddaughters of me
Dresser drawers Vanity for

As a tot, I don't remember a lot
First night that I spent the night
Get in the extra bed Grandma said
She tucked me in with a grin
Again and again I remember then
Sweet dreams Sleep tight Good night

So much to be said
About still having this bed
Take care of who Nurtured you

Their days have gone by
Nurtured kept their furniture
Then a day it came my way
Kids' room now a spare room
As I stood beside that very bed
Grandbabies of me Neat in the suite
Sweet dreams Sleep tight Good night

TRUFFLES SHUFFLES

Glory days that's all
Songs about rain
Siberian Khatru
Her strut how come
In the heart of the usher
Let it burn

My pod shuffles
My brain truffles
Fast forward with a zip
Rewind with a flip
Thoughts shuffle by
In a blink of an eye

Hang tough I've heard that
Sipping on fire I kissed a girl
Show me Thinking about you
Sassafras roots How deep
Is your coming home unhappy

My pod shuffles
My brain truffles
Fast forward with a zip
Rewind with a flip
Thoughts shuffle by
In a blink of an eye

Outcast Iron man
Transistor natural science
Confessions three
Tonight she comes Stir it up
Hell yeah Circus People are strange
Teakbois the life the garden

WORD

Words of word
Words can be heard
Said instead of read
A herd of words without sound
Heard words said in your head
Words intent are to be meant

Read along to a song
Lyrics Poems Jibber
Hearing Feeling Healing
Bringing meaning singing

Dictionary Bound Reference Found
Alphabetical order in order
Equip for a quip to lip
Sound out Spell out
Words make you feel
Happy Sad Mad Real
Rude when a curt tude

Games play Words say
Words dabble in scrabble
Upwords Crosswords Passwords
Jumble Search Spelling Telling

Intellect Dialect Beset
Pronunciations Enunciation
They can hammer grammar
Mark my words Four letter words
Pointed words In other words
Latin words make most words
Silent letters don't make better

CHAPTER SEVEN

ELEVEN SENSES

Feel each real
Shall not a pal
Three prorate eight

GODS BEFORE ME

GRAVEN IMAGE

NAME IN VAIN

HOLY SABBATH

HONOR THY FATHER

SHALL NOT MURDER

COMMIT ADULTERY

SHALL NOT STEAL

BEAR FALSE WITNESS

THOU SHALL NOT COVET

LOVE THY NEIGHBOR

THOU SHALL NOT HAVE OTHER GODS BEFORE ME

Nor beside Me Nor after Me
Never from under Though some think
Some worship leaves and the trees
Most the earth and all it is worth
Easy to see why civilizations rot
Different gods and what nots

THOU be me myself and I
Oh for sure Us We and All
SHALL is absolute no scoot
NOT to forget no means not
HAVE possession regression
OTHER who you think is another
GOD is ABSOLUTE Give a Smile Salute

I'm not sure what the Incas did think
Greekology and their mythology
Mayan calendar a little flounder
Egyptians made their points
Some undug Some a flood
Hindsight is always right
Yesteryears of tears

THOU be me myself and I
Oh for sure Us We and All
SHALL is absolute no scoot
NOT to forget no means not
HAVE possession regression
OTHER who you think is another
GOD is ABSOLUTE Give a Smile Salute

Religion we need a family to be
Believe I say GOD is our every way
He is not a name He is not a title
Name and title Sing at a recital
Your right hand a polite stand
Face the mirror with your heart
It's time we All make a new start

THOU SHALL NOT WORSHIP ANY GRAVEN IMAGE

No disrespect you can always expect
Graven seems like a deep subject
Those days Makes perfect sense
Today it needs an explain
Such an old word today
Like Jesus on the cross
Give idolatry a toss

THOU be me myself and I
Oh for sure Us We and All
SHALL is absolute no scoot
NOT to forget no means not
WORSHIP pray or say any way
GRAVEN means etch and sketch
IMAGE a human eye never spy

An ample example
Six thousand homes
where I have roamed
I can attest To this mess
Mary here Joseph there
Bury who where for what
Jesus in every shape and form
Hebrew doors has some forms

THOU be me myself and I
Oh for sure Us We and All
SHALL is absolute no scoot
NOT to forget no means not
WORSHIP pray or say any way
GRAVEN means etch and sketch
IMAGE a human eye never spy

GOD you see in your every mirror
Face Him every day with a smile
Thank him for your every way
Without a word or pray any way
With no regret See what you get
Life not a fret with His safety net

76

THOU SHALL NOT TAKE GODS NAME IN VAIN

Well God damn We are all out
Try and lie repeat offenders
Surrenders with a Jesus Christ
Without a doubt I called All out
Oh My God with a shout
He has tuned us all out

THOU be me myself and I
Oh for sure Us We and All
SHALL is absolute no scoot
NOT to forget no means not
GOD the One our Father His Son
VAIN has so much blame

Never ever will He ever
Advertise for a rise or surprise
Don't advertise your faith for success
Your success is from your faith
He is the Father of all fathers
Many of us are grounded
Because he is confounded

THOU be me myself and I
Oh for sure Us We and All
SHALL is absolute no scoot
NOT to forget no means not
GOD the One our Father His Son
VAIN has so much blame

If He damned all we said
No one would have a bed
Born with a habit such of this
Seems like the easiest to dismiss
Kiss it goodbye with a teary eye
Get your rate closer to Eight

REMEMBER THE SABBATH KEEP IT HOLY

Saturday was the first day of rest
But now the rest think Sunday best
Sunday fun day with family is best
It is my attest But not for the rest
Not for me to say for you to pray
You and God will figure it out

REMEMBER think and repeat
SABBATH day of rest Calm breaths
KEEP give to receive
HOLY for the Love of God
Everyday is His way

Grill out Chill out Ride it out
You get one day to sleep away
Or make it the day of your way
Be lazy be crazy even if hazy
Say any way you want to say
Thank you for the day
Is the simplest way

REMEMBER think and repeat
SABBATH day of rest Calm breaths
KEEP give to receive
HOLY for the Love of God
Everyday is His way

No way for any to say right or wrong
Family time Alone time Church time
Polite right No contrite or spite
The toll gate how you rate
Below eight un-straight
Bell tolls your soul
before your old

HONOR THY FATHER THY MOTHER AND THY ELDERS

Enormous role out of control
There is three that made you be
No doubt we owe them all a shout
It is not about for you to like it or not
But for you to make your way or not

HONOR love respect
THY is yours and some mores
FATHER A rad dad A bad dad and GOD
MOTHER mom mommy mum for some
ELDERS are the few who walked before you
One day makes them wise to say

If your parents don't lead your need
Turn and learn to be better than them
The father you truly need you can't see
Please and thank you every day
He will guide your way

HONOR love respect
THY is yours and some mores
FATHER A rad dad A bad dad and GOD
MOTHER mom mommy mum for some
ELDERS are the few who walk before you
One day makes them wise to say

Don't disrespect with your life retrospect
Their mind time is now past prime time
Your chance More than happenstance
If you raise a child improved of you
You too will have a different view
Circle of life without strife

THOU SHALL NOT MURDER

A brother or of another
One day a brother's hand
maybe your helping hand
That brings you to a stand
Fend ourselves defend ourselves
Eat what you need Meat or a treat
It is never right when out of spite

THOU be me myself and I
Oh for sure Us We and All
SHALL is Absolute no scoot
NOT to forget no means not
MURDER the BURNER

Put your rage in a cage Write a page
Submit your complaint without an ain't
Profess or confess The fewest words best
The end of the day It is always His way
Accident prone Accident unknown
Karma bad luck in front of a truck
The fall is much farther without
a regular call to our Father

THOU be me myself and I
Oh for sure Us We and All
SHALL is Absolute no scoot
NOT to forget no means not
MURDER the BURNER

Free will to kill
Always pays in other ways
Your life will never go your way
and will end an unordinary way
There shall always be a price to pay
Like Judas noose When broke away
Jagged rocks Excruciating splay on display

THOU SHALL NOT COMMIT ADULTERY

Atrocity of pain
Murderess act of fact
To rip someone's heart apart
Promise God to do your part
Stand before Him with your Heart

THOU be me myself and I
Oh for sure Us We and All
SHALL is absolute no scoot
NOT to forget no means not
COMMIT done went an did
ADULTERY attractor distractor retractor

O go on and live your life
Thinking you are alright
Sins pay along your way
Health Wealth and stealth
Is a gauge that you pay
No one commandment
Can ever be broke alone

THOU be me myself and I
Oh for sure Us We and All
SHALL is absolute no scoot
NOT to forget no means not
COMMIT done went an did
ADULTERY attractor distractor retractor

Imagination of another's way
Flirting always undeserving
Wink an eye Crack a smile
Stare the back or a rack
Signal wiggle or jiggle
Showing what ya got
Porn the pot of rot
Love who you got

THOU SHALL NOT STEAL

That everyone wrongly gains
What everyone wrongly loses
Really stealing from ourselves
Struggling to pay for ourselves
A role that is out of control
The only person not a thief
An infant in a pumpkin seat

THOU be me myself and I
Oh for sure Us We and All
SHALL is absolute no scoot
NOT to forget no means not
STEAL is for real a BIG deal

You get what you need
Won't work If you don't work
No Slow ride Low ride Free ride
Life's meter is not a parking meter
No free button but an easy nothing
What you give you receive just believe

THOU be me myself and I
Oh for sure Us We and All
SHALL is absolute no scoot
NOT to forget no means not
STEAL is for real a BIG deal

Pick a pocket or trick a pocket
Slip something into your pocket
Discount without a finger count
Extra drink at the fountain drink
Skip a tip after an extra trip
Want a deal for half a meal
Loaded dice is never nice
Cheating a reading
Has only one meaning

THOU SHALL NOT BEAR FALSE WITNESS

I'm not sure what more
one can say about a lie
the vocabulary of this kind of witness
is more than a thesaurus before us
Ninety-one noun-verb of words
Untruth of each listed beneath
With so many words we say
Liar liar your pants on fire

THOU be me myself and I
Oh for sure Us We and All
SHALL is Absolute no scoot
NOT to forget no means not
LIE under Honesty of Truth

To be an adult and continue to lie
Deceive and receive without reprieve
Apologize Confess Forget the rest
Wash Rinse Repeat Retreat
When you get there
You may well see
A glassy stare
From up
there

THOU be me myself and I
Oh for sure Us We and All
SHALL is Absolute no scoot
NOT to forget no means not
LIE under Honesty of Truth

You don't let a child lie
Where is your ample example
Your trouble is more than double
Regret is to forget you are His child
There is no excuse for your abuse
Repeat offenders have no defenders
To say or do raise your right hand too

83

THOU SHALL NOT COVET

Merchants advice sinvice
Enticement Entrapment
I want this I want that I want all
Life is enough a brawl in thrall
To have to do with all else too
A mess needs addressed

THOU be me myself and I
Oh for sure Us We and All
SHALL is Absolute no scoot
NOT to forget no means not
COVET want lust and greed

It is a two=way street
Double line the equal sign
Just because you are a have
Have nots have it hard enough
With all your flair and no care
Your boasting is just the same
Causation collaboration
Coconspirator in a mirror

THOU be me myself and I
Oh for sure Us We and All
SHALL is Absolute no scoot
NOT to forget no means not
COVET want lust and greed

Great what you got and what not
The end of your day gets thrown away
Cash and jewelry spent without care
House is someone else's home
But your apologies for the grief
Will be needed for your relief
Share with your neighbor
Spare your neighbor
Grace in place

LOVE THY NEIGHBOR

Jesus said Love everyone as I have loved you
A neighbor like you He never saw come true
Have nothing nice to say So walk away
But to reach out too choke you out
My imagination makes me smile
While on my way with no say

LOVE Jesus command
THY be me myself and I
Oh for sure Us We and All
NEIGHBOR Any Human sort

To erupt your neighbors abrupt
Makes you a disrupter interrupter
Talk to our Father before you bother
The wrong will be right without spite
No need to see or say outcome way
If you don't get your way His way
Ask yourself about yourself
What to do to better too
Smile wave walk away

LOVE Jesus command
THY be me myself and I
Oh for sure Us We and All
NEIGHBOR Any Human sort

As I attest at the beginning best
The ways of these days understood
To say I love my neighbor is a lie No lie
Now two are broke No joke
Here is another Attempt without contempt
Just respect each other is of another way
Smile and wave as you pass each day

CHAPTER EIGHT

MIX OF OTHER SIX

Whoa is me poetry
Poetry without
Whoa is me
Myrics
Self reflects
I'm just a dude
Never trying to be rude

HYPOCRITE

HELEN RED

BKOO BKEE

I'M NOT UPTIGHT

SHELF YOURSELF

MIND VISION TELEVISION

THRILL NOT THE KILL

NOT MY ALGORITHM

NEW SOUND FOUND

YOU TOO CAN TOO

HYPOCRITE

Hypocrites always hands on their hips
Nothing kind from their lips wide hips
Shooting from the hip with your lips
Does more than sink ships
or breaks sails over rails
Kafaws of your flaws

What you see is what you get
Embrace your face Can't replace
Daily check so you don't forget

Lawmakers flaw makers
Lawbreakers jail makers
Always for thee not for me
Scoop fools of loopholes
Contradiction mantradiction
Chronic ironic truant incongruent

What you see is what you get
Embrace your face Can't replace
Daily check so you don't forget

Tartuffe and aloof yell from the roof
Fractions of your actions divided so small
So we learn to ignore and try not to snore
Your way in your day not for anyone to say
Hype is your life we won't recite to be polite

HELEN RED

Helen lying in bed in the red
Needing to keep the family fed
What the heck living check to check
No thrill with bills No magic pills
Such a fret living Helen debt
Debit cards just don't go far

Helen Red laying in bed
Helen Red new blue shoes
Helen Red more than can afford
Helen Red wants more for sure
Helen Red is never alone
We all live like Helen Red

Underwater In over her head
Recession Depression Bed impression
Black Friday Red Saturday Blue Sunday
Mail a check before the paycheck
Rubber check to float the boat
Money spent before the rent

Helen Red laying in bed
Helen Red new shoes blues
Helen Red more than can afford
Helen Red wants more for sure
Helen Red is never alone
We all live Helen Red

Every holiday and other days
Special of the day A special day
Ads subtract Retailers in the red
Deals Meals Fishing reels Red heels
In the black Stocks bounce back
Helen Red bounces back to bed

BKOO BKEE

My Love
Turn Turn Turn
Good Samaritans were two
Paper-wrapped candy cigarettes
Grandma's house Butcher shop
Parallel paths never stopped
Maybe seen maybe spoken
Separated and unbroken

First sight was right
Hidden tribe the guide
Sunshine raised the day
Life's fight we did not fight

Hunks Foxes
Immature minds
Ask for One Took it all
Coiled wire tethered wall
Folded note Teacher read
Legacy careers No life fears
Needles and nails History sails
Love paused never stopped

Second sight out of sight
Hidden tribe the guide
Sunshine raised the day
Life's fight we did not fight

Time ticks Nearing paths
Humbled aged and wised
Friend of a friend
Accepted again
A text a call reliving it all
Fast forward Play paused
Each had three Now of six
Made into a perfect mix.

I'M NOT UPTIGHT

A kid's day of fray they say
When their zinger is a ringer
You are so UPTIGHT
For three days away
Somber and pondered

I'm not uptight
You have no idea
I was fun when I was young
You made me who I am
A responsible one Son

Since the very first day
I worked every day for you to say
You are so uptight in a fight
Everyone knows about your fun
Sharing your every move
With evidence to prove

I'm not uptight
I partied hardy
Scenes unseen never seen
Left some marks at parks

My past went fast didn't last
A lot of tales with no trails
A picture or two Not a few
No way to investigate any state
Proof gone aloof and poof

SHELF YOURSELF

What's in your soul when you stole
What do you feel when you steal
It's not a rush Hide your blush
Your song is all wrong

Feelings Bringing Meanings
You telling You knew
Wrong gong songs

You ignore more and more
Yet you were already caught
With your first thought
Reactions of your actions
Add up as you age up
A price to pay everyday
SOMEDAY

Meanings Bringing Feelings
Sense of wrong Gongs
Intense sense defense

Honest thoughts trot
Speaking without thinking
You have to try to make lies
Forethought of every thought
You are caught
You feel what you speel
Nitwit Dimwit Halfwit Knowit

MIND VISION TELEVISION

Entertainment here
In my domessphere
Imagination Animation
Channel surfing Rip tide ride
Sounds that jingle and mingle
Surround a sphere is neat to hear

Imagination not just for fun
Mental vision made television
Make-believe and fantasy
Outside the box Rocks

Close my eyes can be a surprise
Nightdream a vague stream
Daydream Floggin in my noggin
Never a need to see to believe
Pull the brake for a break
Create and make not fake

Imagination not just for fun
Mental vision made television
Make-believe and fantasy
Outside the box Rocks

Art al le carte Wall waterfall
Rhyme in time with time on time
Formulate calculate propagate
Color schemes Movie scenes
Photograph memory graph
Stories of yore amore gore

THRILL NOT THE KILL

Breezy day sway away
Invisible leaves in the trees
Crows squawk Distant turkey talk
A tattle tail Barking above a trail
Hot or cold Any drink is a stink

The clothes the gear
Slinging arrows through the year
An arrow flight the end of light
Apologies said Family fed

Hour to sunrise
Five feels like three
Bright trails by closed eyes
Distant red lights snapping twigs
First one Tenth one just the same
Two hearts rushing Ones gushing

The clothes the gear
Slinging arrows through the year
An arrow flight the end of light
Apologies said Family fed

Breakfast sausage cookie snacks
Copious jerky ziplock sacks
Football into basketball
Graded and traded ours best
Biggest racks some with facts
No more shotgun window racks

NOT MY ALGORITHM

I write what I write
I write how I rite
I write when I right
I write where I wright
Rhymes Poems Lyrics

I see your music box
I've peeked into your box
I see rocks in your music box

Verse in a box
Chorus in a bocs
Bridge in a boks
Repeat in a boxs

Fit the mold to get sold
Music is Art is music
Structured creativity
Is only part of the art
It is a box of the same rocks
Go kick rocks This one rocks
Originality without finality

Pop in a bocks
Country in a boqs
Rap in a bachs
Rock in a box

People in the throws
Don't know Blinded so
Climb into a windowless box
Thinking smarter than art
Leaving the art apart
Outside the box
Box of rocks

NEW SOUND FOUND

What sounds are found
With the form of paraforms
Landscape make Oscilloscope slopes
Highs and lows shows the flow
Words sound free for which key
Count of lines for rhythm time
Words more Syllables galore

Every Good Band
Deserves Fans and Cash
Digits count Notes mount

The center line of each line
left or right words count
Three is C Six be E see
You will get the gist
With a letter list
Affords chords

Turned around
Topsy turvy curvy
Flip flop don't stop

Context not complex
Subtext of the context
Quotes notes for folks
Words heard Sound around
Break it down The art found
Myrics reflex of text reflects

YOU TOO CAN TOO

What shapes
will your myrics make
Paraforms of informs
Should be easy to do
If you are True

A blank page
Marginal margins
Refrains constrains
Center justify your try
Describe what you see
Your words you know
Will make the flow
A simple penny
Describe with
Your eye

Where to look
Reference book
Dictionary bound
Definitions found
Spellings sound
Proof adds to
the truth

Each paraform
Alone on its own
Holds what you told
Problem solve Resolve
New words and phrases
Shapes more than vases
Sharpened mind you'll find

WHAT I HOPE FOR MOST

Is the art to grab another heart
To find other art that they part
Songs never seem to be wrong
None of vain Nor two the same
Some have signs of the same lines
Thought-provoking fine-line timeline
Unanswered questions suggestions
Imagination fascination
Lyrics Poems Myrics
A reflection without deflection
Thought Interpretation Association
Preponderance of ponder and wonder
Shapes of Round Taper and Waves
Newel Barrel Vase Deco base
Random seems learning means
My life art the biggest part
Words that say pray play
No room to assume
You can guess
I guess